D0409585

N16875

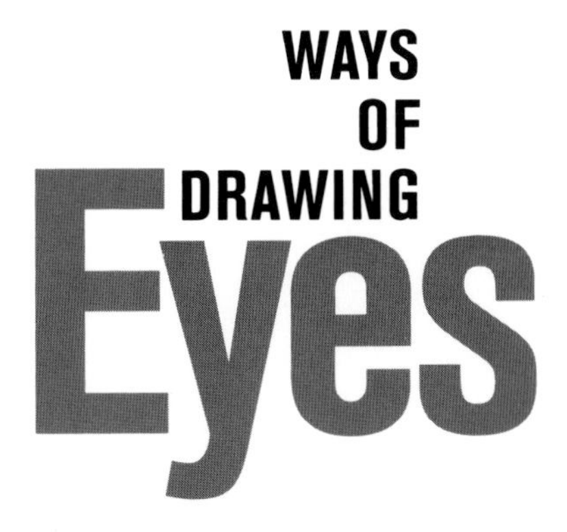
WAYS
OF
DRAWING
Eyes

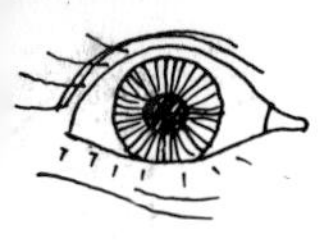

“Day after day,
never fail to draw something
which, however little it may be,
will yet in the end be much,
and do thy best.”

Cennino Cennini c.1390

WAYS OF DRAWING Eyes

CASSELL

A guide to expanding your visual awareness

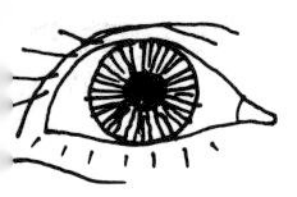

Ways of Drawing Eyes,
a guide to expanding
your visual awareness

This edition first published in Great Britain 1996 by Studio Vista an imprint of the Cassell group

British Library Cataloguing in Publication Data
A catalogue record for this book is available from the British Library

ISBN 0-289-80159-1

Produced, edited, and designed by Inklink, Greenwich, London, England.

Consultant Artists and Editorial Board
Concept and general editor, Simon Jennings
Main contributing artists, Robin Harris and Roger Coleman
Additional artwork, Albert Jackson, David Day, Alan Marshall
Anatomical artist, Michael Woods
Art-education advisor, Carolynn Cooke
Design and art direction, Simon Jennings
Text editors, Ian Kearey and Albert Jackson
Historical research, Chris Perry

Typeset in Akzidenz Grotesque and Univers by Inklink
Image generation by T. D. Studios, London
Printed by South Sea International Press, Hong Kong

Cassell Publishers Limited
Wellington House, 125 Strand
London WC2R 0BB

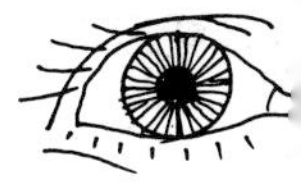

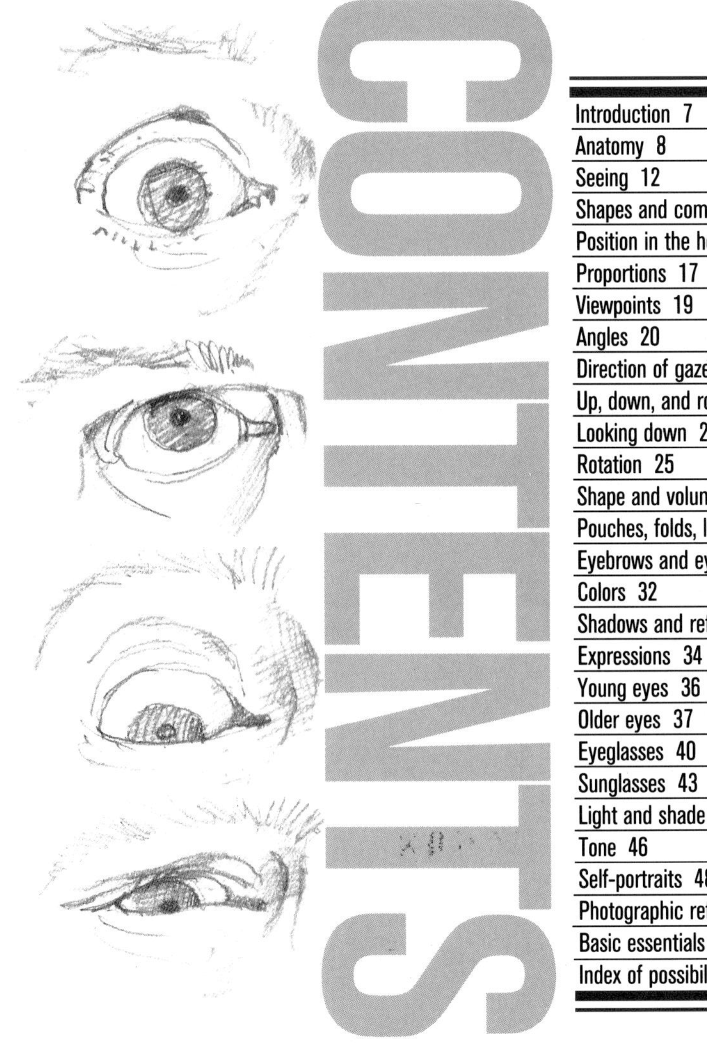

CONTENTS

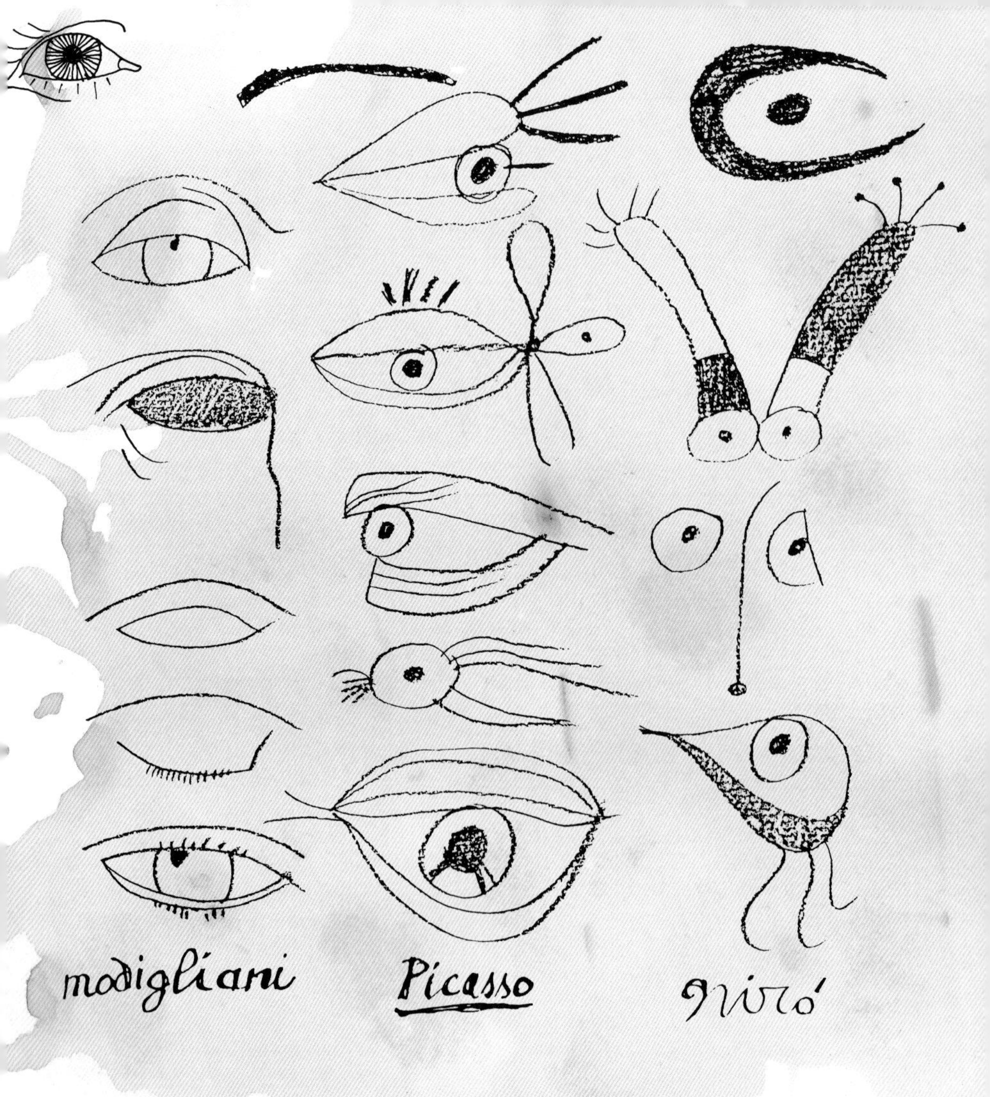
modigliani
Picasso
Miró

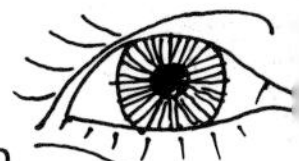

Introduction Drawing is a universal means of communication. The young child's desire to make marks is followed by drawings that are full of confidence in their ability to pass on visual information. The themes and ideas in this book are intended to help restore that confidence in making marks, and to enable you to work openly and creatively – bridging the gap between wanting to draw and being able to do so successfully. The **"Anatomy"** section shows you how the many components of the eye and its surrounding structure can be used to express a wide variety of non-verbal messages and emotions. **"Seeing"** gives you examples of how to use the formal, visual elements of line, tone, proportion, shape, and texture to convey the different expressions and character of the owner of the eyes you are drawing. An important part of drawing is becoming familiar with the many different types of equipment and materials you can use; **"Basic Essentials"** guides you through the different ways of looking, to help you choose the appropriate mediums for your subject. The **"Index of Possibilities"** demonstrates that the urge to draw is common to all cultures and traditions, and offers ideas for inspiration and exploration.

The most meaningful and interesting drawings come out of the tension between your personal response to all these influences and factors, and the way it is communicated through the process of your work. This book, rather than providing a formula for the representation of eyes, will help you to develop that response through an exciting variety of visual ideas.

ANATOMY

The anatomy of the eye In the days when the study of anatomy was still in its infancy, artists like Leonardo da Vinci filled pages of notebooks with sketches of eyes, from bare spheroid eyeballs to the enigmatic, coded gaze that eventually graced the Mona Lisa. You do not have to go to such obsessive lengths, but a working knowledge of the eye's anatomy will undoubtedly improve your powers of observation, and from that, your art.

It pays to develop a broad understanding of how an eye fits in the skull and how its appearance is affected by the muscles and skin that surround it. The individual components – the eyeball, socket, muscles, eyelids, eyebrows, and lashes – appear to be very simple, but the interplay and relationship between these various components can be extraordinarily subtle,

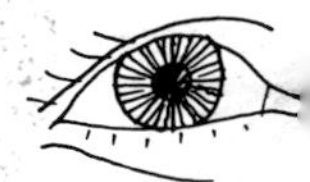

making the human eye capable of a wide range of movement that, in turn, conveys a whole gamut of emotions. The eyes are not called the "mirrors of the soul" for nothing – no other feature can express so much with such little variation.

And there is little or no room for error when trying to convey these subtleties in a drawing. We are so used to reading the messages sent out by eyes, that even the slightest misplacement of what seems an insignificant line can completely change our reading of a portrait.

When drawing a model or a self-portrait, notice how the smallest shift in position will alter the whole mood of the eyes; understanding why this is so, and how the eyes move and are controlled, goes a long way toward being able to convey mood and character accurately.

Background
Detail from *Anatomie de l'Homme,* 1821-32 by Jules Cloquet.

Below
Section of the human head, 1489-92 by Leonardo da Vinci.

Bony ridge
This varies from person to person. It often casts deep shadows.

When drawing an eye, remember that it is not a flat image pasted to the front of your face. It is a three-dimensional object set within a hollow eye socket.

Muscles
The whole eye area is covered by a single, thin, circular sheet of muscle that closely follows the form of the skull. The muscles that rotate the eyeball are too deep to be seen by the artist; the bones and skin, and their relationship to the eyeball, are the more significant factors. However, what the muscles do to the eye and its surrounding tissue is very important, especially in terms of facial expressions.

Eyeball
The eyeball is a moist sphere, with its own shadows and highlights. Note with care the relationship between the eyeball, lids, eyebrow, and muscles. Also, the little bump where the tear duct opens should be noted. The tear duct has shadows and highlights, too.

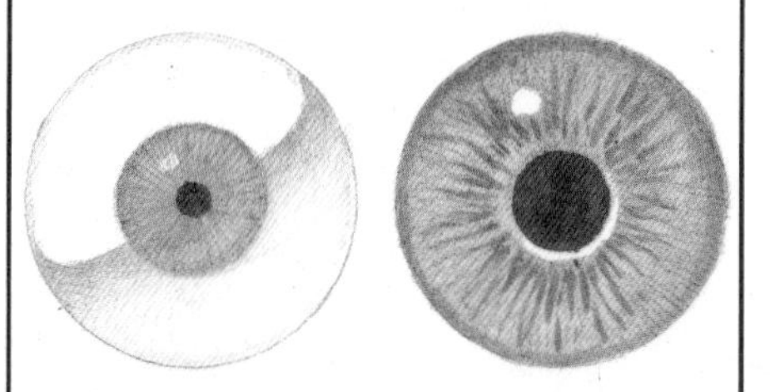

Raised eyebrow
When the eyebrow is raised in surprise or delight, it appears to travel up the forehead, emphasizing the upper bony ridge of the eye socket.

Eyeball and socket
With deeply set eyes, you can see clearly the entire rim of the socket beneath the skin. This is especially noticeable on older people.

Changing shape of the brow ridge
The outer edge of the ridge is relatively sharp, but it tends to thicken and become rounded as it approaches the nose.

Stretched skin
With increasing age, the skin stretches and sags, almost covering to upper eyelid. Note, also, the thickness of both eyelids.

The lower ridge
On some people, the lower ridge of the eye socket hardly shows externally, especially when pouches or "bags" form below the eye.

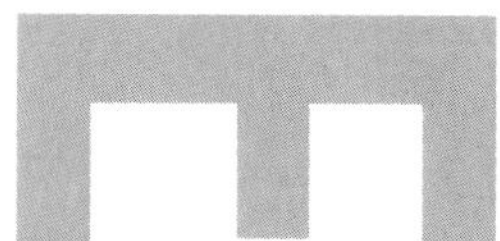

Look them in the eye As a species, we use our eyes to convey an amazing number of subtle messages. With our gaze alone, we can tell someone that we love or loathe them, scorn or fear them, and all mostly on such a subliminal level that we can barely suppress the messages we are sending. Is it any wonder, then, that many of us find it difficult to look another person in the eye and run the risk of giving them the wrong impression or, on the other hand, of picking up signals that may confuse or intimidate us? In most cultures, it is considered unacceptable to stare at someone, in case we embarrass them.

With so many inhibitions on eye contact, it is hardly surprising that artists often find the drawing of eyes so difficult; they just haven't had the opportunity to look hard or long enough.

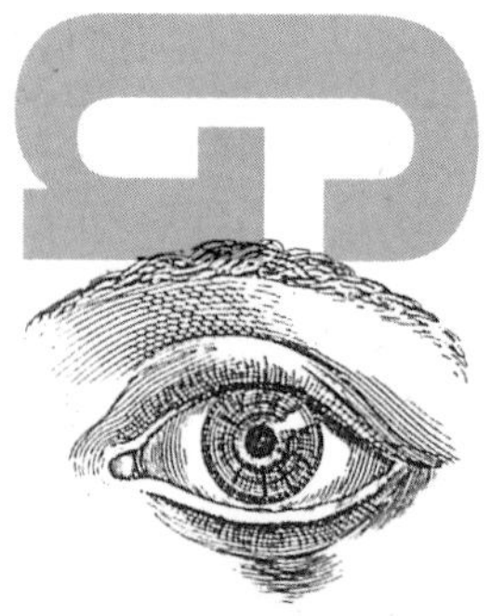

Rather than cause embarrassment, start by using magazines and books as sources of reference. However, it is practically impossible to see any detail in printed images of eyes, and the best you can hope for in this situation is to familiarize yourself with the basic proportions of the eyes in relationship to the face.

A better solution is to draw your own eyes in a mirror. Here, you have the advantage of being able to concentrate on your drawing for as long as you wish, with plenty of opportunity for experimentation with a variety of mediums. Nevertheless, you can only draw your own eyes from one viewpoint. Eventually, you will have to pluck up the courage to persuade friends, family, and even strangers to pose for you, if you are ever to meet the challenge of observing and drawing eyes.

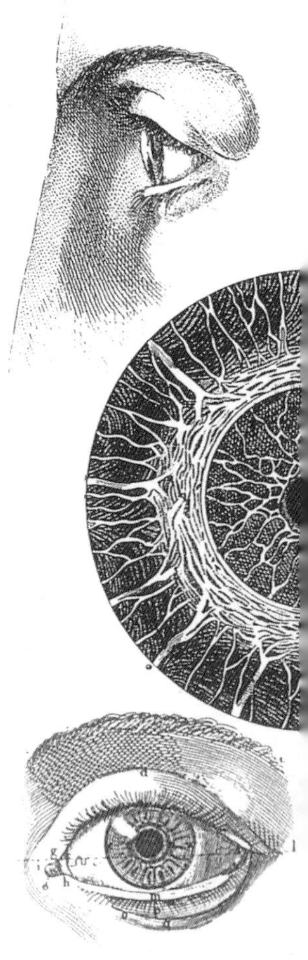

There are no hard and fast rules on how to draw eyes, but these pages of observations will help you to see the components of the human eye more clearly. And there's no such thing as step-by-step solutions to successful results. Every artist must develop his or her own style and approach through practice and experimentation.

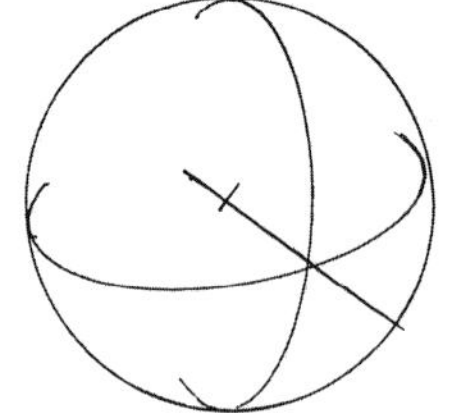

Spheres
The human eyeball is approximately spherical, but only a small part of the sphere is visible.

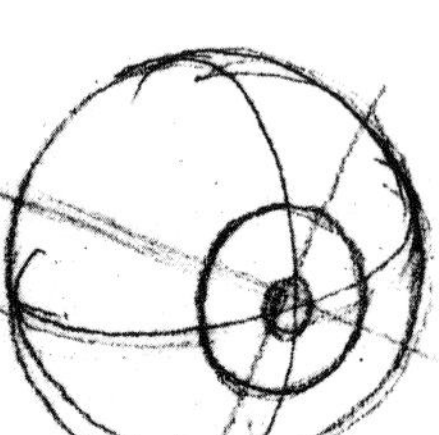

Positioning the pupil and iris
Intersecting horizontal and vertical lines mark the position of the pupil and iris.

Iris
The iris is circular when the person you are drawing is looking straight at you. When seen from the side, the iris forms an ellipse.

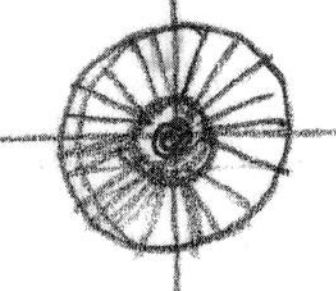

Frontal view
When seen head-on, the intersecting lines form a cross at the center of the eyeball.

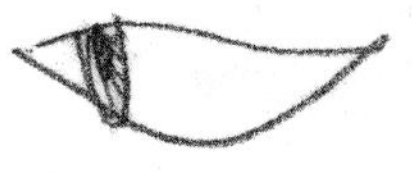

Oblique view
In an oblique view, these straight lines become elliptical.

Eyelids
The eyelids, which follow the curvature of the eyeball, vary in shape from person to person, and with changing facial expressions.

Bottom eyelid
The bottom eyelid often adopts a gentle S-shape, particularly when the eyes are narrowed.

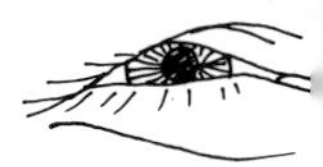

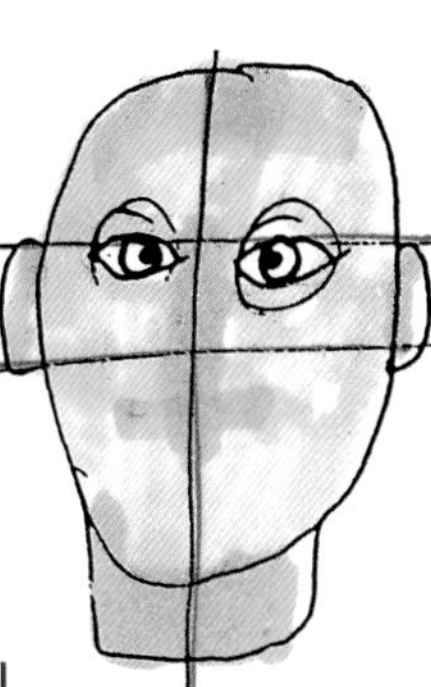

Eyebrows
The hairs of the eyebrows do not grow randomly. Note the direction of growth and how the hairs tend to follow the line of the bony ridge beneath.

Consistent gaze
Make sure the positions of the pupil and iris are consistent in both eyes when drawing a portrait. This ensures that the subject will be looking at a particular point in space without squinting.

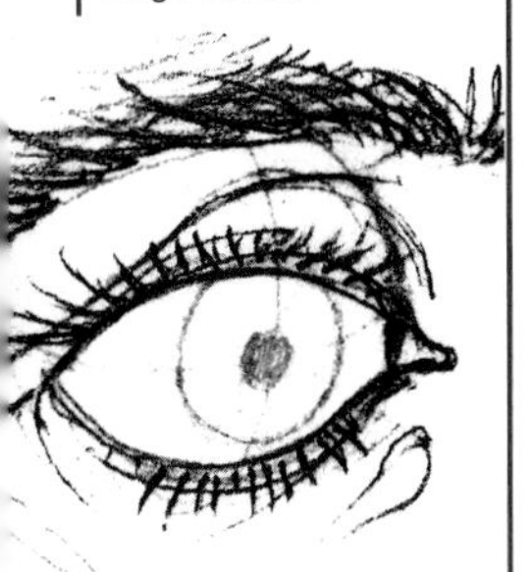

Eyelashes
The lashes curve away from the eye, and usually taper sharply. Those on the outer edge of the upper lid tend to angle away from the nose and are normally longer than the others.

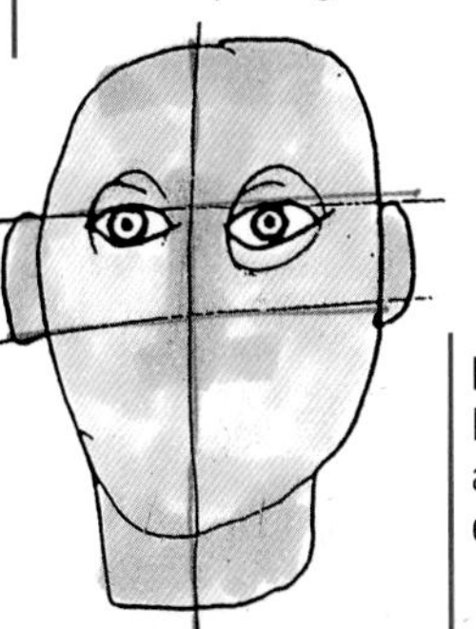

Bone structure
Draw in the areas to be shaded. These must appear to follow not only the curvature of the eyeball itself, but also that of the underlying skull.

POSITION IN THE HEAD

Vertical positioning
These full-face and profile views show that the eyes are about midway between the top of the skull and the jaw-line. A common fault among children and inexperienced artists is to set the eyes too high in the head.

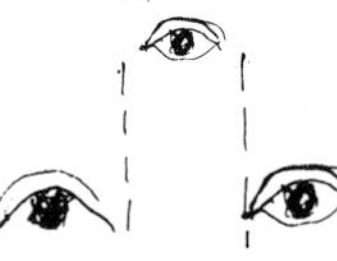

Distance apart
When plotting the position of the eyes, allow approximately one eye-width between them.

Schematic drawings
Children plot the elements of a face according to their relative importance, with no attempt at actual proportion or real-life positioning.

A baby's eyes are well below the center of the face, and its nose is relatively short. In an adult, the eyes are at the center of the face, and the nose is longer in proportion.

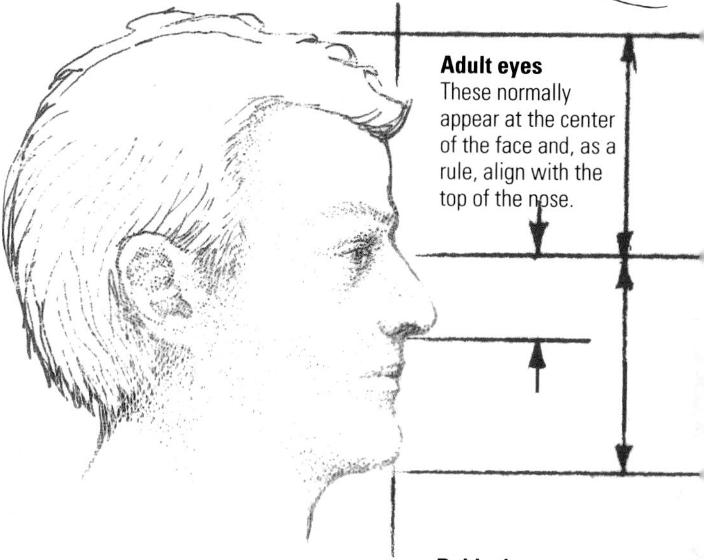

Adult eyes
These normally appear at the center of the face and, as a rule, align with the top of the nose.

Babies' eyes
As well as appearing to be in the lower half of the face, their positioning is also emphasized by the proportionally smaller nose and mouth.

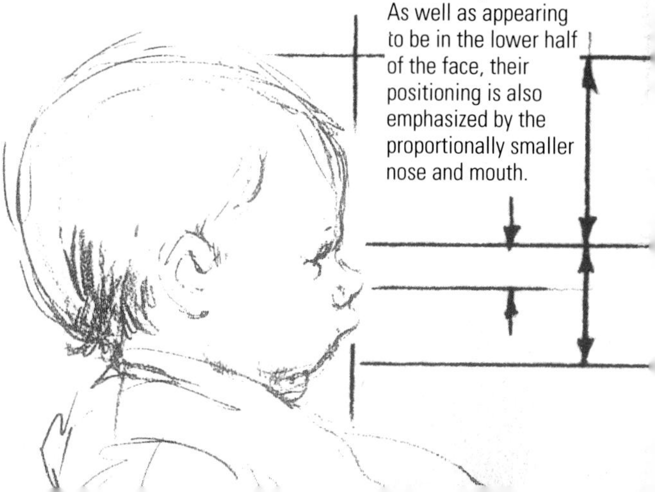

Relative sizes
The iris is fully developed from birth and never gets any larger. As a result, the eyes of a baby or young child appear proportionally larger than those of an adult.

While it is relevant to generalize about age-related variations of proportion and the position of features, it is worth remembering that individuals also vary considerably one from another. This variation may well be an evolutionary trend to help distinguish friend from foe. Unlike other animals, humans rely heavily on vision rather than smell for recognition.

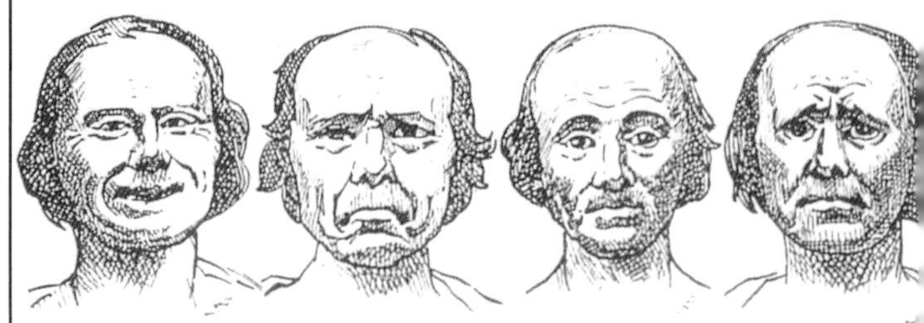

Physiognomy
The eyes play the most important role in these characteristic expressions, based on real-life observations from a 19th-century anatomical study of physiognomy (study of facial features).

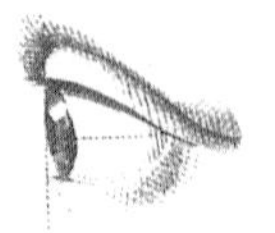

Capturing likeness
The eyes are the most expressive features of the face. Even tiny inaccuracies in observation can make it impossible to achieve a satisfactory likeness to the sitter.

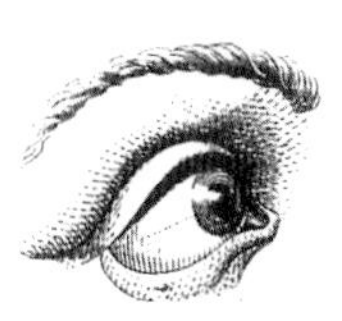

Pen, ink, and wash studies
The artist has studied the models from a variety of viewpoints. Note the use of watercolor washes that add color and modeling to the drawings.

Despite their relatively sophisticated treatment, these three portraits embody all the basic "rules" governing shape, positioning, and proportion of eyes.

When drawing heads at an angle, remember to also tilt the eyes on the same plane.

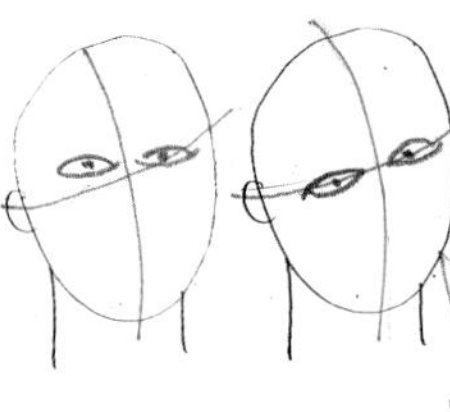

Tilting heads
These pen-and-wash studies (left and above right) show the eyes accurately observed in the same plane. Note also the dominance of the upper eyelids when viewed from this angle.

Inclining heads
Studies from "The Theory of the Art of Drawing" (right) from *The Iconographic Encyclopedia of Science, Literature and Art,* 1851.

Three-quarter view
A three-quarter view of a head reveals how the outer edge of the eye socket is set back, so that the cheekbone appears to project below the eye. The bony ridge above the socket also projects sharply, forming the lower edge of the forehead.

We are intuitively aware of how eyes should appear, even when they are averted. We can therefore judge with some accuracy when an artist makes a pair of eyes look slightly crossed or divergent.

Slightly different
When a pair of eyes are turned aside, they may no longer look exactly the same, simply because one has to turn a little more than the other, in order to focus on a distant object.

The appearance of human eyes changes when they open and close, or when they rotate upward, downward, and from side to side. The shape of the eye will also change considerably, depending on the viewpoint from which it is being drawn.

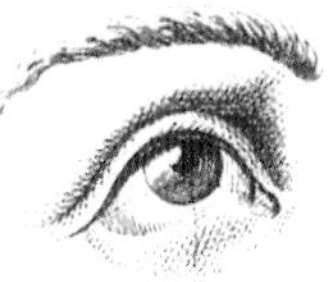

Looking up
Wide-open eyes looking up at the artist are bright and open to mood and expression. They can reveal a lot about the personality of the model.

Looking down
Hooded, downward-looking eyes can appear dark and mysterious, providing little information about the mood of the sitter.

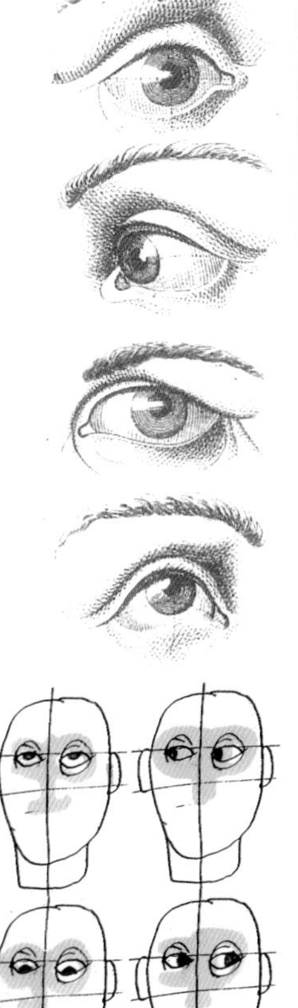

Rotation of the eyeball causes changes in the eyelids and the surrounding skin.

Upward rotation
Upward rotation stretches the lower lid and the associated areas of skin.

Downward rotation
More of the upper eyelid is revealed with downward rotation, that contracts the lower lid to little more than a narrow ridge.

Side-to-side rotation
This movement has little effect on the eyelids, but can contract or expand the area of the tear duct (lacrimal caruncle) in the corner of each eye.

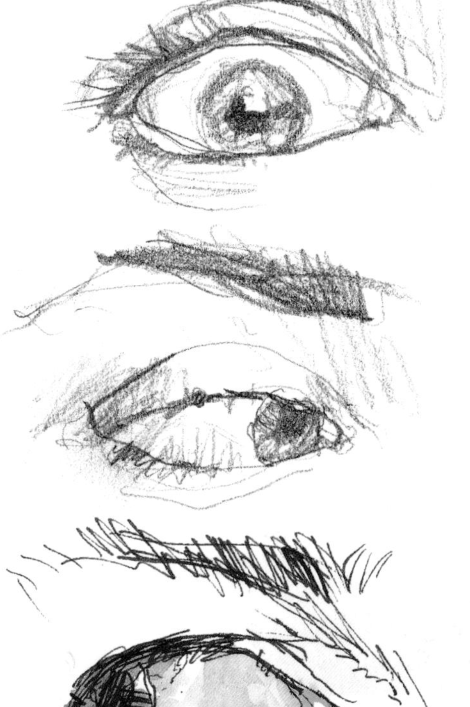

Changes in the eyelid
As the eye moves from side to side, the shape of the top eyelid changes as the slightly bulging cornea distorts it.

Whether the eyes are open or closed, the spherical nature of the eyeball is evident when drawing portraits in profile. The same shape is discernible from face-on, but you may have to resort to shading to interpret it.

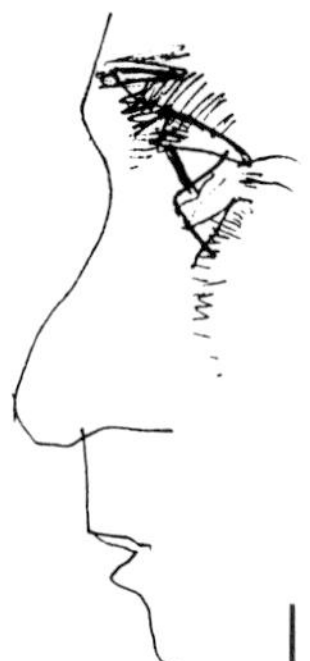

Eyes in profile
When the eye is closed, the lid emphasizes the the spherical nature of the eye. When the eye opens, the folded lids tend to mask much of the sphere.

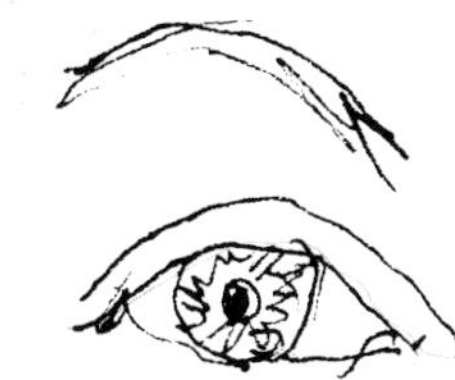

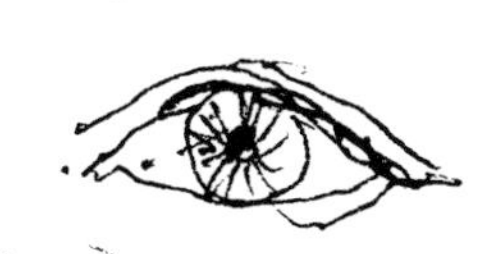

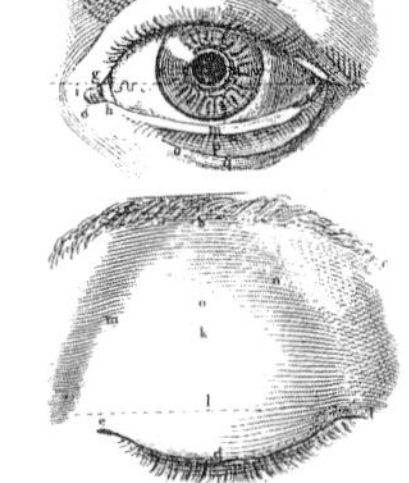

Distinctive cornea
The bulging corneas can often be seen clearly under the closed eyelids.

Cornea
The cornea is a protective membrane that projects slightly, forming the anterior surface of the eyeball. The iris and pupil are behind the transparent cornea.

POUCHES, FOLDS, LINES, AND LIDS

Except for the color of the iris, the eye itself is a fairly standard organ throughout the human species. It is the context of the eye – folds of skin, eyelashes, and eyebrows – that gives each pair of eyes their unique character.

Pouches
The pouches below the eyes are often most noticeable in a smiling face. Though not particularly flattering to the sitter, they can bring a face to life when observed and drawn with care.

Folds
Asiatic eyes have a distinctive fold of skin on the insides of the top lids.

Lines
Whether you call them "crow's feet" or "laughter lines," the creases at the sides of the eyes are a great indication of character and personality, and imply mood and expression.

Eyelids
The outer limits of the upper eyelid often tend to overlap the lower lid. The upper lid is always the larger of the two and has a much greater range of movement.

Eyebrows and lids
With some people, there is practically no gap between eyelids and eyebrows.

Drooping eyelids
The slack skin that partially covers the eyelids is usually a sign of ageing.

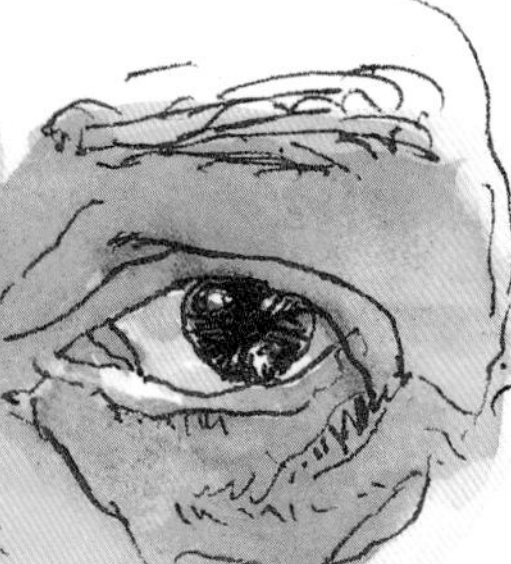

Large eyelids
Larger-than-average eyelids give the eyes a languid appearance.

Inclining forward
When the head is inclined forward, the eyelids are less visible.

Invisible eyelids
The eyelids are sometimes almost invisible, especially when squinting into bright light.

The upper edges of the eye sockets are marked by the eyebrows; note how the socket edges actually pass across the line of the eyebrows, which appear darker at that point. Eyebrow hair also tends to grow vertically at the nearest point to the nose.

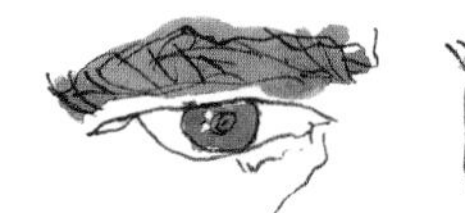

Eyebrows and expression
Straight, upturned, and beetling eyebrows create very different expressions.

Shape and direction
The shape of the eyebrow and the direction of the eyebrow hair help to describe the underlying structure.

Eyebrow hair
Individual eyebrow hairs, that are longer than eyelashes, tend to grow upward and outward. As a person ages, eyebrow hair often grows longer and more unruly.

Eyelashes mark the edge of the eyelids. They provide interesting textural detail, and draw attention to the eyes themselves. Long, dark eyelashes are generally considered attractive, and are often emphasized with make-up.

Expressions of emotion
Smiling, frowning, and other expressions of emotion wrinkle the skin surrounding the eye, and alter the relationship of the eyelids.

Random spacing
Eyelashes are somewhat randomly spaced along the lid, and tend to clump together.

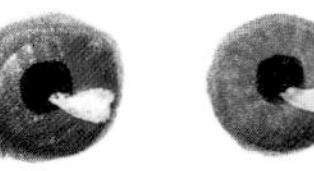
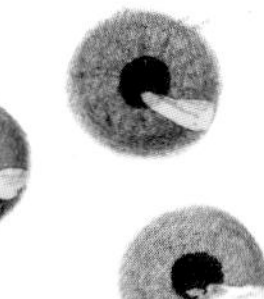

Iris color

This is never a flat tint, but is subtly and individually modulated; it is often darker on the outer edge. The iris is textured, with ridges and valleys.

We all know that the color of irises varies from person to person, but what about the so-called "whites of the eyes?" This is not an expression to be taken literally – hold up a white card to someone's face to see!

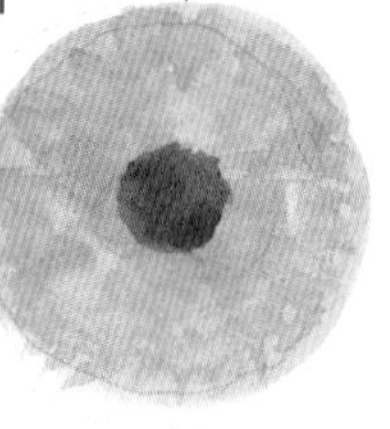

Dilation and contraction

The size of the pupil affects the apparent color of the eyes. The pupil changes in size, depending on light levels. When dilated, due to a low level of light, the pupil is large and the area of colored iris is correspondingly small. In bright light, the converse is true.

The "whites"

The color of the eyeball ranges from bluish-white in babyhood to yellowish-brown in old age.

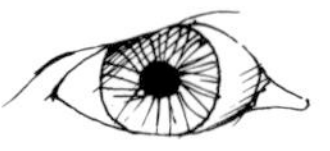
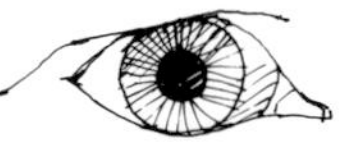
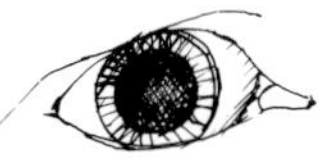

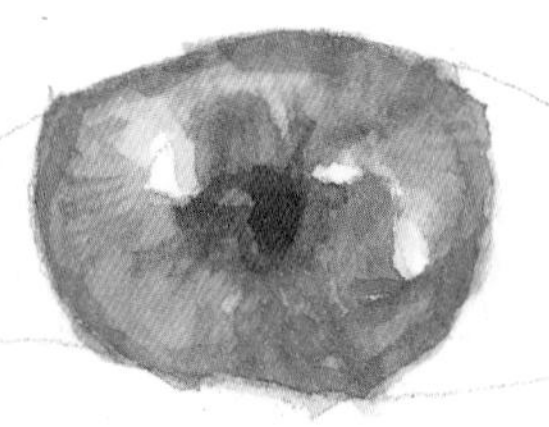

Tear ducts

The red of the tear ducts can be a useful reference point when drawing eyes from life.

The smooth, wet surface of the eye produces mirror-like reflections, but because it is convex, the reflected images are distorted. Shadows cast by the eyelids help describe the spherical shape of the eyeball.

Highlights
Whether large or small, highlights and reflections will follow the contours of the surface of the eyeball.

To show the curvature
Shade the eyeball lightly, so that it still appears to be white, and draw in the shadows cast by the upper lid. The colored iris is darker, and you can hatch it with radial lines. The pupil, being a hole, is quite black.

Reflections in the pupil and cornea
The inner edge of the pupil has its own highlight. The cornea, being a transparent bubble protruding from the surface of the eye, displays reflections similar to the spherical eyeball.

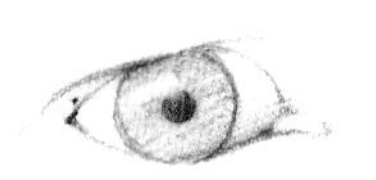

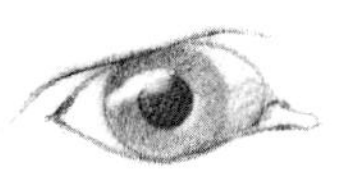

Stylized reflection
A simple, stylized reflection drawn in the form of a curved wedge across the iris makes the eye look shiny and helps define the shape. This reflection should be applied to both eyes at the same angle.

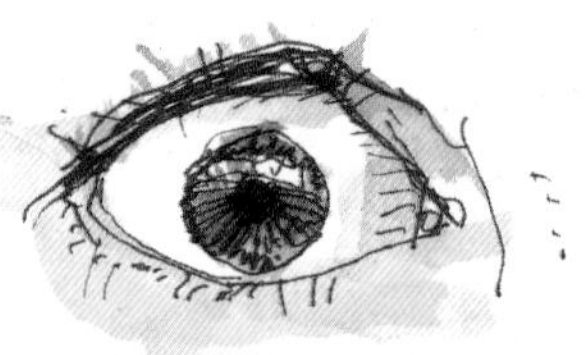

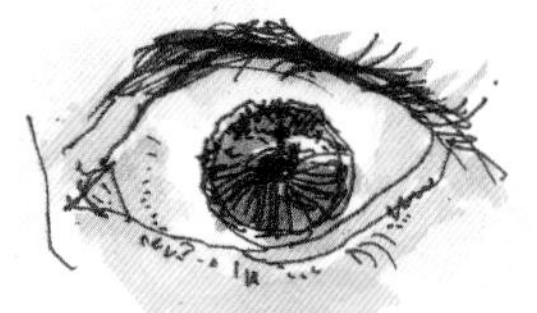

It is possible to recognize emotion in a drawing of eyes, even without including any other features. Astonishment or surprise, for example, are indicated when the eyebrow and eyelid are raised, revealing the white of the eye above the pupil. A startled expression seems exaggerated when the subject is looking down, because the eyes tend to open even wider.

Other emotions clearly communicated by the eyes are those of disbelief and, of course, laughter and happiness.

Disbelief
A narrowing of the eyes suggests a quizzical mood. Squinting into strong light produces a similar effect. Note also the lowered eyebrows.

Happiness
Laughing or smiling creates half-closed eyes with raised eyebrows. Look out for laughter lines which are the creases on each side of the eye.

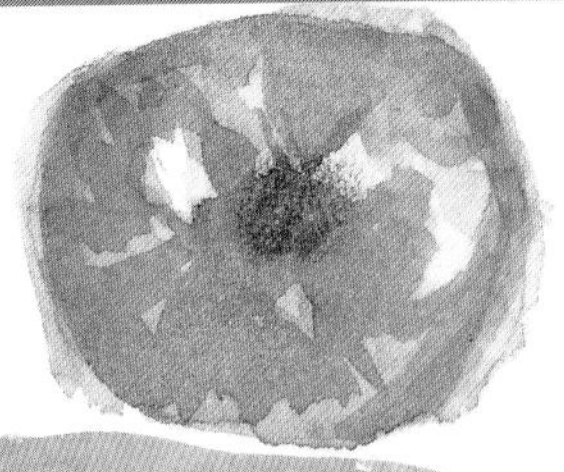

Like the rest of our anatomy, eyes change a great deal as we get older. For an artist it is both a pleasure and a challenge to depict the extremes of youth and old age.

Wide-eyed innocence
You can see in these watercolor sketches how the eyes seem to dominate portraits of babies and young children. They are not only proportionally larger than adult eyes, they are also bright and colorful, and surrounded with fresh, smooth skin. Close-up studies will reveal that children often have exceptionally long eyelashes that emphasize the eyes still further.

Mere suggestions
Eyes change gradually over the years, parallelling the changes in the whole face. In this craggy, sculptural face, the eyes can hardly be seen, and are merely dark holes under heavy brows.

As people get older, the folds of the upper eyelids droop and rest on the eyelashes, pouches develop below the eyes, the radiating lines at the corners of the eyes deepen, and the frown lines between the eyebrows become permanent.

Receding eyes

As many people age, their eyes seem to shrink into the increasingly complex folds and creases around them. The iris is less prominent and paler in color. Sometimes, the sockets become clearly defined as the eyes retreat into them.

Muscle forms
The concentric form of the muscle that overlaps the eyeball starts to show more in later life, and creases and lines can begin to appear along the concentric texture.

40 EYEGLASSES

Eyeglasses can be used as props in very theatrical ways, and can enliven drawings of faces.

Off the nose
In the left-hand drawings, the eyeglasses are pulled down, which dramatically focuses attention on the eyes.

Looking over
A similar, but somewhat superior, expression is achieved in the right-hand picture by the subject looking at the viewer over half-glasses.

Distortion from eyeglasses
From certain angles, eyeglass lenses distort the eyes, making them appear to be on a different plane to the rest of the face; it's an effect worth noting when drawing people wearing eyeglasses.

Reflection in eyeglasses
Because they are curved, eyeglass lenses give a distorted, wide-angle reflection, with objects appearing smaller than they would in a mirror with a flat plane.

By association, the wearing of sunglasses is somewhat sinister. Apart from preventing eye-to-eye contact, sunglasses resemble the dark, blank, eye sockets of a skull – a symbol of death in every culture.

Tinted lenses
Drawing a hint of the eyes behind dark glasses suggests translucent, tinted lenses.

Dark glasses
Very dark sunglasses are an effective way of drawing attention to the eyes; because the eyes are invisible, we cannot be sure who or what the person is looking at, and the person's emotions or mood are a blank page.

44 LIGHT AND SHADE

Establish the direction from which the light is falling, and begin by plotting the main illuminated areas before drawing in the smaller areas that are in shadow. The eyes and their surrounding area comprise the most expressive region of the face, and tiny changes completely alter the expression or likeness of the drawing.

Contrasts
The darker the skin, the whiter the eyes will seem by comparison. Look for the way darker skin affects the tints to be found in the whites of the eyes.

Shade
A strong side light will put the eyes in shade, increasing their dramatic intensity.

Hatching
Shade an area by drawing parallel lines close together.

Crosshatching
Overdraw hatched lines at an angle, to create a darker tone.

Shading
Create tone by shading with a soft pencil, or try a combination of the above techniques.

Solid shadows
Create areas of shadow with solid tone. Under certain lighting conditions, you will be unable to see highlights in the eye, due to the deep shadow cast by the eyelid and brow.

Dot and stipple
Create subtly modulated areas of tone by stippling with the point of a pen; the closer the dots, the darker the tone.

Try to create the effect of light and shade by using these shadow and shading techniques, either individually or in combination.

Throughout this book, you will have noticed that the artist has applied color to many of his drawings, to give them volume, density, and the illusion of light and shade. Don't be afraid to experiment with brush-drawing and color or tonal washes to extend your range.

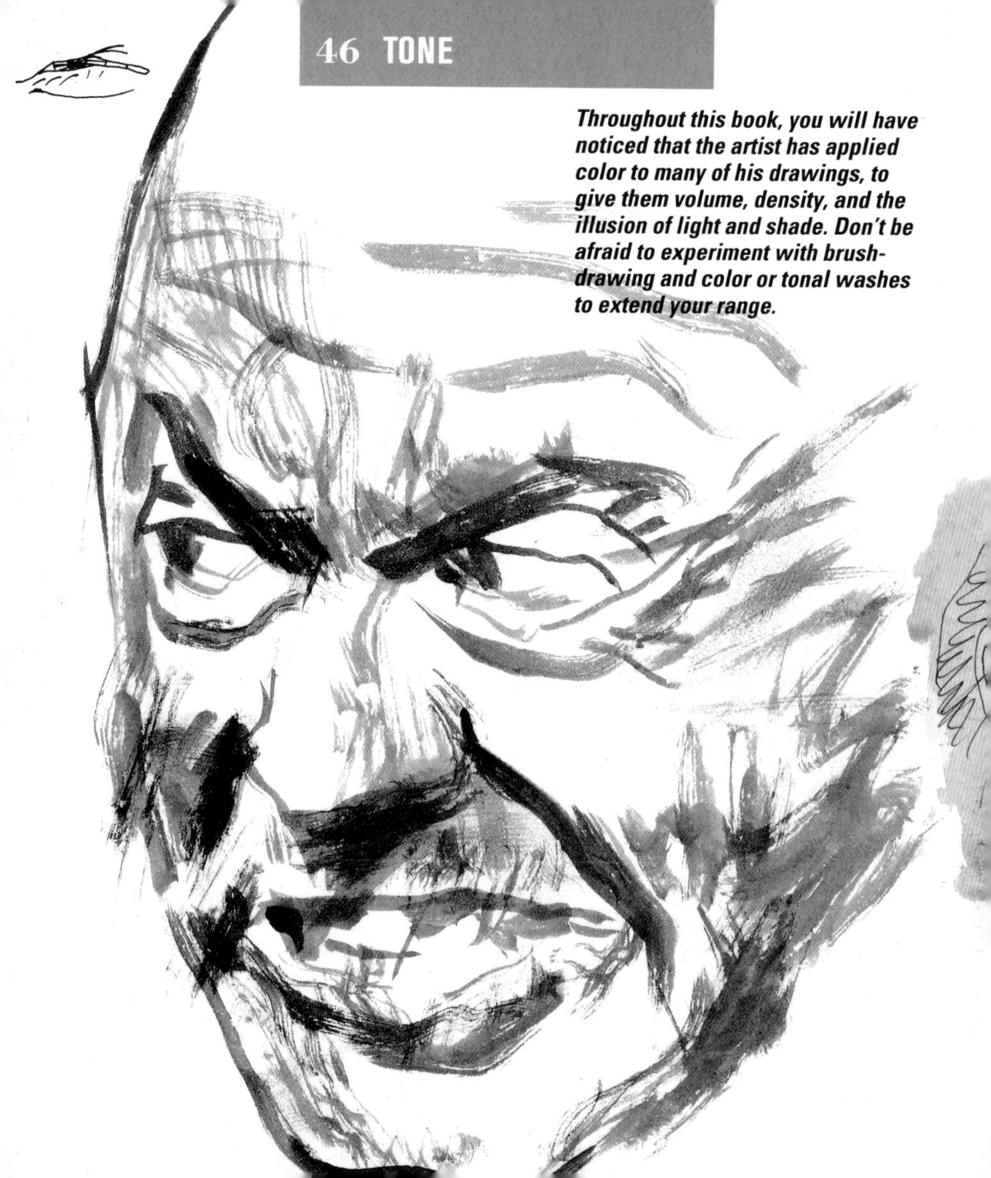

Choosing a suitable medium
These dramatic expressions (left and below) demonstrate that it is important to choose a drawing medium that produces the required effect. Drawing directly with a brush forces you to adopt a lively, fluid style, and bold pen-and-ink hatching (below) makes for a drawing full of tension.

Washes
Create tone and areas of deep shadow in your drawings (right) by applying transparent washes over initial linework.

As an art form, self-portraiture has immense appeal. It is an opportunity for self-analysis; a chance to study a reflection that one sees but fleetingly in a mirror. The penetrating gaze that is common to nearly all self-portraits no doubt reflects the intense concentration of the artists wrestling with the problem of capturing an image whilst looking deeply into their own eyes.

Mixed media
Ballpoint and fiber-tip pens were used in combination with red conté crayon to create this expressive self-study.

Soft pencil
Note particularly the way the artist has rendered light and shade to create depth and modelling in this pencil study.

Pencil studies
These self-studies rely on the use of line and hatching only, to create the sense of tone and depth.

Fine-point, fiber-tip pen
As it is impossible to vary the line width with this type of pen, the artist has sought to achieve light, shade, and dimension, by using hatching, crosshatching, and overdrawing.

The majority of artwork in this book has been drawn from self-studies and live models, as first-hand experience is the best way of learning about the subject in front of you. However, like many professionals, you may sometimes have to resort to photographic sources for inspiration and reference .

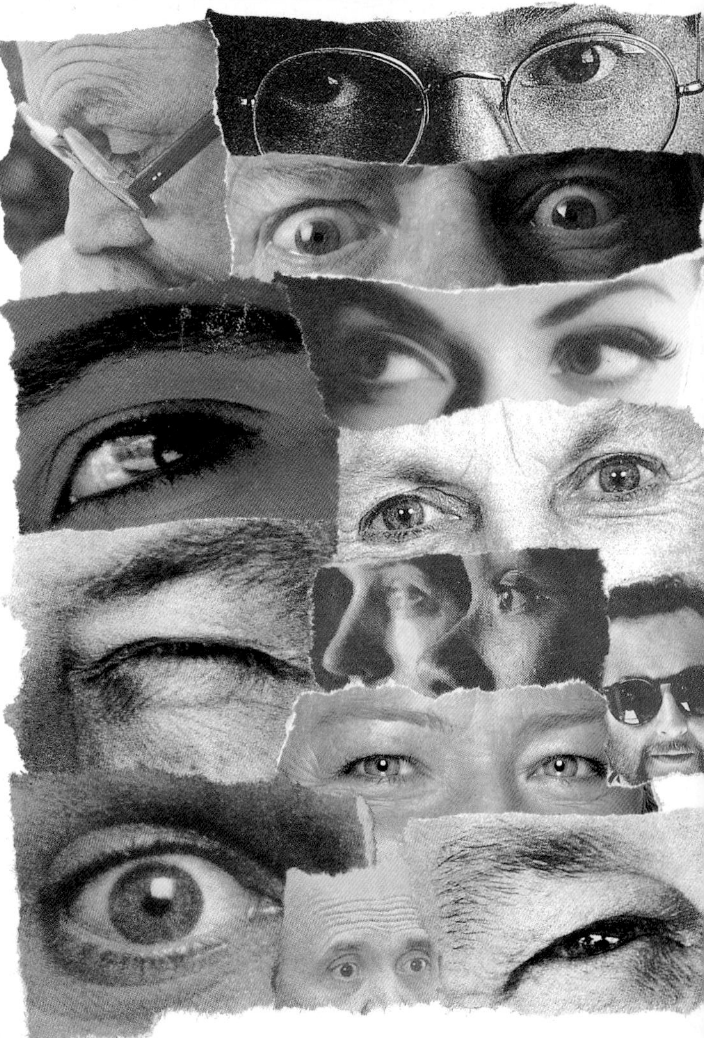

Building a picture library
Professional artists and illustrators often use photographic references to help them with their work. It is a good idea to build a visual resource of found images, filed by subject, to help you in the same way. Most of the eyes on this page were either photographed by the contributors or clipped from old newspapers

Beware of distortion

Tracing from a photograph may seem like an easy way to make a drawing, but it does not necessarily lead to an accurate representation. Although it may be entirely convincing as a printed photograph, the same image may look distorted when reduced to a drawn outline. This is most often the result of lens distortion, that artificially stretches or foreshortens an object in camera. As a result, when using photographs for reference, you must be willing to make alterations to achieve correct proportions.

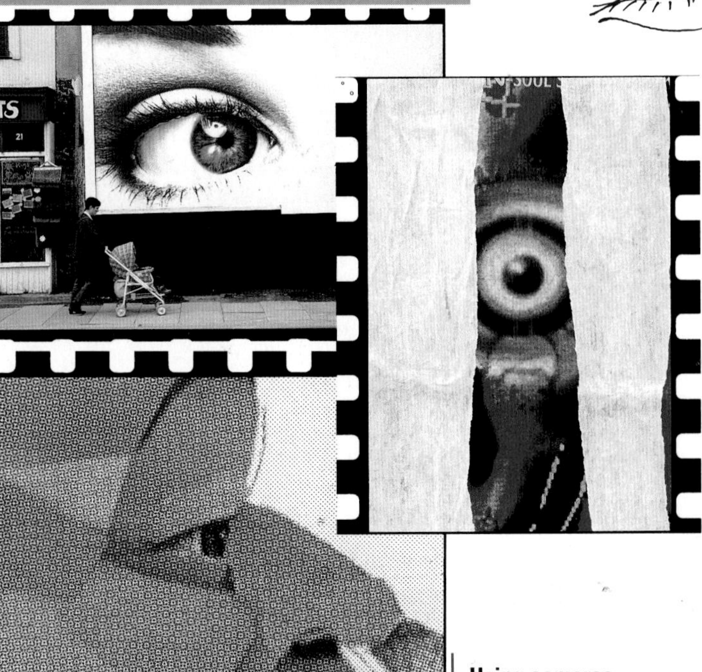

Using cameras

Photography may be your only realistic alternative for that particularly hard-to-find pose. It can freeze a fleeting movement into a ready-made two-dimensional image. Many professional illustrators use "instant" cameras for quick results.

BASIC ESSENTIALS

The only essential equipment you need for drawing is a pencil and a piece of paper. But, as your experience grows and your skills develop, you will hopefully discover your own drawing style. As this happens, you will probably develop a preference for using particular art materials. The visual information in this book is the work of several hands, and you will have seen references to a variety of art terms, materials, and techniques, some of which may be new to you. The following is a glossary of useful information that relates to the artwork featured in this book.

MATERIALS

Graphite pencil
The common, "lead" pencil, available in a variety of qualities and price ranges. The graphite core (lead) is encased in wood and graded, from softness to hardness: 9B is very, very soft, and 9H is very, very hard. HB is the middle-grade, everyday, writing pencil. The H-graded pencils are mostly used for technical work. For freehand drawing work, start around the 2B mark.

Colored pencil
A generic term for all pencils with a colored core. There is an enormous variety of colors and qualities available. They also vary in softness and hardness, but, unlike graphite pencils, this is seldom indicated on the packet.

Watercolor pencil
As above, except water-soluble and capable of creating a variety of "painterly" effects, by either wetting the tip of the pencil or working on dampened paper.

Conté crayon
Often known as conté pencil, and available in pencil or chalk-stick form. Originally a proprietary name that has become a generic term for a synthetic chalk-like medium, akin to a soft pastel or refined charcoal. It is available in black, red, brown, and white, but is best known in its red form. A traditional and well-loved drawing medium.

Steel-nib (dip) pen
The old-fashioned, dip-in-the-inkwell pen, a worthy and versatile drawing instrument. You will need to experiment with nibs for thickness and flexibility. They can take a while to break in and become free-flowing in use. However, the same nib can give a variety of line widths, as the

artist changes the pressure on the pen.

Fiber-tip pen
Available in a variety of tip thicknesses. The ink flows smoothly, and fiber-tips make good drawing pens. When the ink runs out, they are useful for creating drybrush effects (see below).

Drawing ink
There are a variety of inks available, from water-soluble, writing (fountain pen or calligraphy) inks to thick, permanent, and waterproof drawing inks. India ink is a traditional drawing ink; it is waterproof, very dense, and dries with an interesting, shiny surface when used thickly. Drawing inks are available in a range of colors, and can be thinned down with water for washes.

Paper
Varies enormously in type, quality, texture, manufacture, and price. Paper is graded from smooth to rough, and is either smooth (hot-pressed, or HP), medium (cold-pressed, or CP), or rough. The smoothness or roughness of a paper is known as the "tooth." For example, the tooth of a watercolor paper is generally more marked, and rougher than that of a cartridge paper for drawing. The tooth of a paper will influence the way that a medium reacts to it.

TERMS

Drybrush
A drawing effect created by using a sparsely-loaded brush, often with watercolor, or dry, fiber-tip pen. Drybrush allows the texture of the paper or any drawing beneath to show through.

Mixed media
A drawing made using two or more materials, for example, graphite pencil used with watercolor pencil.

Line drawing
A drawing made up purely of lines, with no attempt to indicate shadow or darker areas through shading or hatching.

Brush drawing
A drawing made with a brush.

Wash
The free application of a transparent color or tone to a drawing, usually applied with a paintbrush.

Shading
An indication of shadow or dark areas in a drawing, made by darkening the overall surface of the area, often by rubbing.

Tone
The prevailing shade in a drawing, and its comparative dullness or brightness.

Highlight
The lightest point in a drawing. This is often the point where a light strikes an object, such as a reflection in an eye or on a surface. This can be done by leaving the surface of the paper unmarked.

Hatching
An illusion of shadow, tone, or texture in a drawing, indicated by lines.

Crosshatching
An illusion of darker shadows, tones, or textures, indicated by overlayering hatched lines at differing angles to each other.

Parallel hatching
Shadows, tones, or textures, indicated by drawing lines next to one another.

Dot and stipple
An illusion of darker shadows, tones, or textures, indicated by small dots, usually made with the pointed tip of the drawing instrument.

POSSIBILITIES

INDEX OF POSSIBILITIES There are many ways of looking at the world, and there are as many ways of interpreting it. Art and creativity in drawing are not just about "correctness" or only working in a narrow, prescribed manner; they are about the infinite ways of seeing a three-dimensional object and setting it down.

In the earlier sections of this book, the consultant artists demonstrated the different approaches to drawing a specific subject. Their examples show how each has developed a personal way of seeing and setting down eyes.

The following section of images is intended to further help you discover and develop your own creativity. It is an index of possibilities: an indication of just some of the inventive and inspirational directions that creative artists have taken,

and continue to take. This visual glossary demonstrates how the same subject can be treated in a variety of ways, and how different cultures and artistic conventions can affect treatments.

In every culture and age, symbols and simplified images are vital factors in communication. The earliest cave drawings reduce the forms of men and animals to the basics, and tell an immediate story; similarly, modern advertising campaigns and computer-based, corporate trademarks depend on our instant recognition of simplified forms. The graphic images in this section show how the artist's eye and hand can produce universally understood forms in all human societies.

A major part of artistic and technical development is being aware of, and open to, possibilities from outside your chosen sphere. To that end, the images in this section use a wide variety of materials and techniques. They may not all be pure "drawing," but each one expands the boundaries of what is possible, and provides new ways of seeing and interpreting eyes.

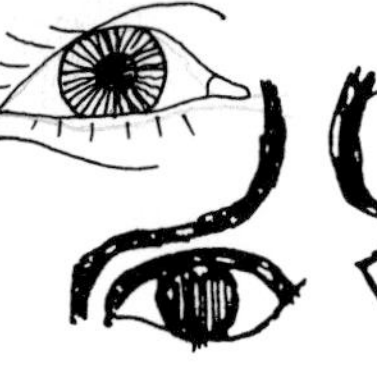

The Boxing Children
Detail, Greece, c. 1500 BC.
Wall painting

Eye of the God Horus
Egypt, c. 2500 BC
Wall painting

Head of Medusa or a Gorgon
Detail from the Temple of Sulis Minerva. The Roman Baths, Bath, England, 200-300 AD
Carved stone

The Singer-priestess Anhai
Egypt, c. 2000 BC
Ink on papyrus

Satyr Mask
Greece, c. 800 BC
Terra-cotta copy of a linen-and-plaster original

Noble Ladies of Mycenae
Greece, c. 1300 BC. Wall painting

Sculptured Vase
Greece, c. 600 BC
Paint on clay

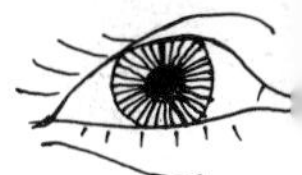

The Virgin
Detail from
Hagia Sofia
Turkey, late
13th century
Wall painting

Head study for Leda
Leonardo da Vinci
(1452-1519). Italy,
c. 1505-7. Pen and ink
over black chalk

Head of a Female Saint
Detail from a
Crucifixion
England, c. 1250
Wall painting

Head of a Man
Albrecht Dürer
(1471-1528)
Germany, 1505
Pen and ink

Self-portrait
Albrecht Dürer
(1471-1528)
Germany, 1500
Oil on canvas

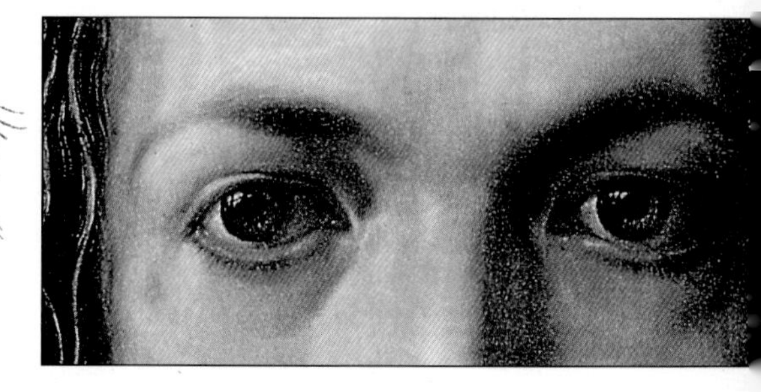

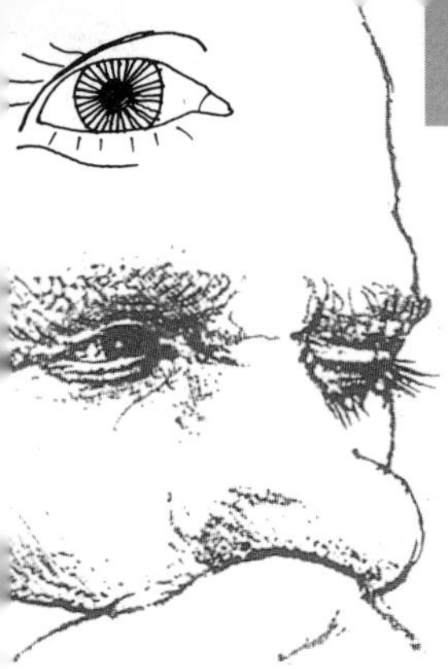

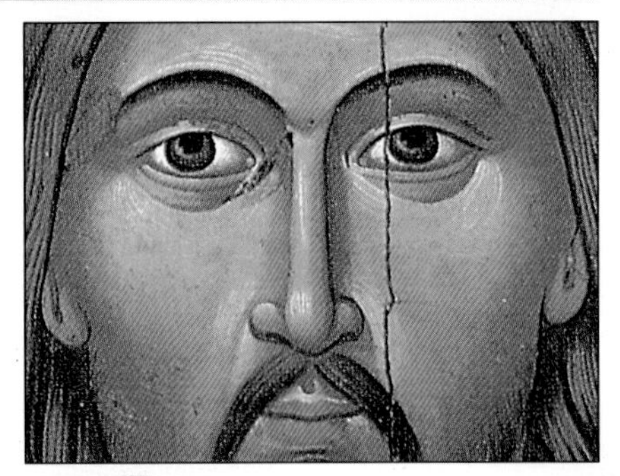

Christ Pantocrator
Church icon
Bulgaria, early 18th century
Gouache on wood

The Judas Kiss
Detail
Hans Holbein the Elder (1460-1524)
Germany, c. 1510
Oil on wood

Head of an Archer
Hans Holbein the Younger (1497-1543)
England, c. 1530
Crayon

Pectoral with a Border of Eleven Heads
Symbol of divine kingship
Nigeria, 16th century
Carved ivory

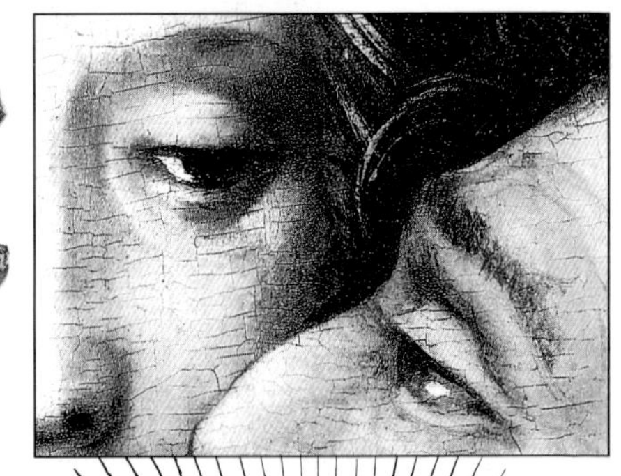

Self-portrait
Peter Breughel the Elder (1525-69). Belgium, c. 1567
Pen and ink

The Weeping Virgin
Bulgaria, 1847. Engraving

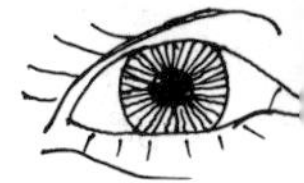

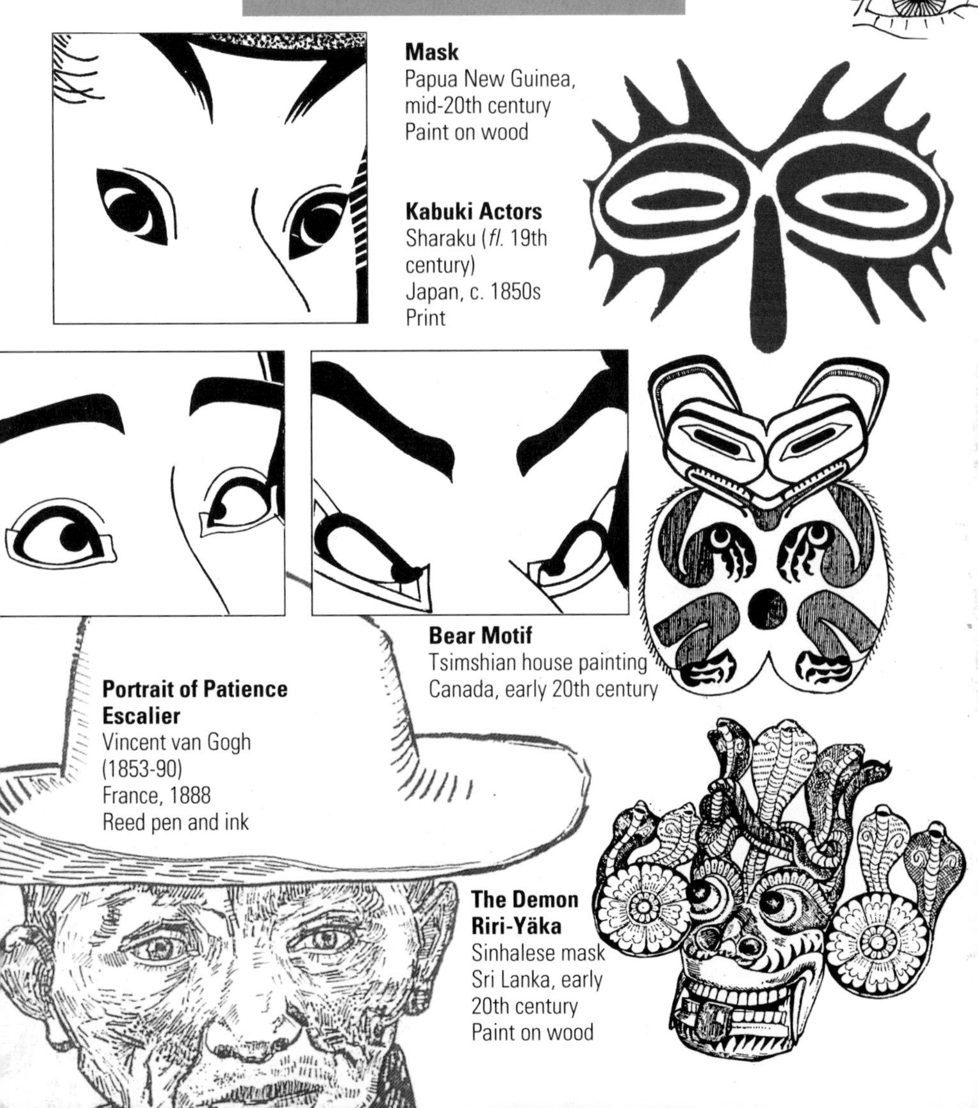

Mask
Papua New Guinea,
mid-20th century
Paint on wood

Kabuki Actors
Sharaku (*fl.* 19th
century)
Japan, c. 1850s
Print

Bear Motif
Tsimshian house painting
Canada, early 20th century

Portrait of Patience Escalier
Vincent van Gogh
(1853-90)
France, 1888
Reed pen and ink

The Demon Riri-Yäka
Sinhalese mask
Sri Lanka, early
20th century
Paint on wood

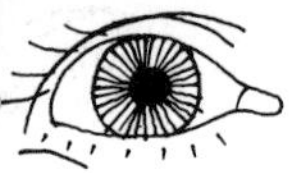

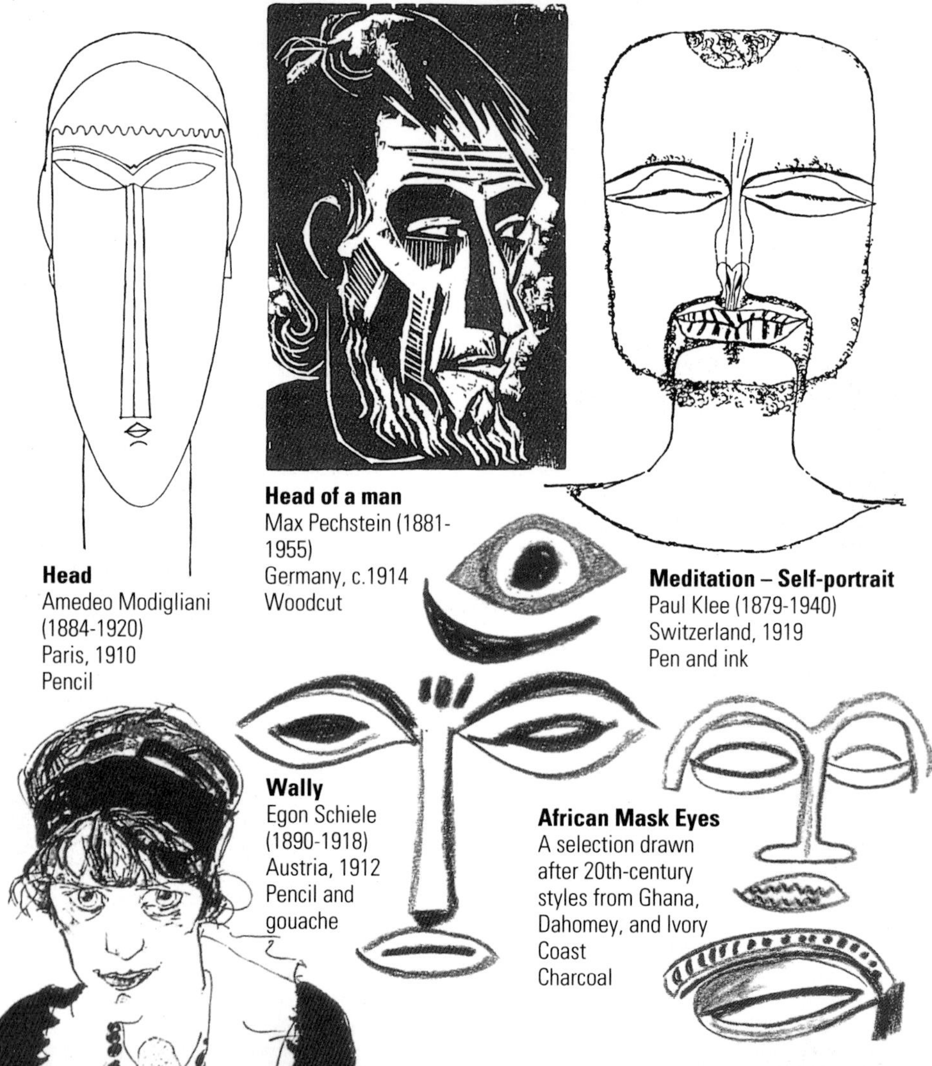

Head
Amedeo Modigliani (1884-1920)
Paris, 1910
Pencil

Head of a man
Max Pechstein (1881-1955)
Germany, c.1914
Woodcut

Meditation – Self-portrait
Paul Klee (1879-1940)
Switzerland, 1919
Pen and ink

Wally
Egon Schiele (1890-1918)
Austria, 1912
Pencil and gouache

African Mask Eyes
A selection drawn after 20th-century styles from Ghana, Dahomey, and Ivory Coast
Charcoal

Hand and Eye
The artist's device
Eric Gill (1882-1940)
England, 1908
Woodcut

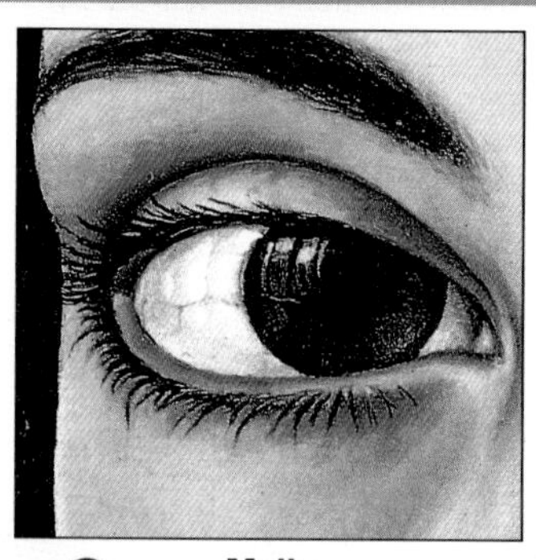

Maika
Detail
Christian Schad
(1894-1982)
Germany, 1929
Oil on canvas

Madonna and Child, with Base
Detail from *The Game*. Eric Gill
(1882-1940). England, 1919. Woodcut

Betty Boop
© King Features Syndicate, Max Fleischer
(1883-1972). USA, since 1930. Animated
cartoons and comics

The Homely One
Paul Klee (1879-1940)
Switzerland, 1922
Pen and ink

Frühlings-Messe der Kunstgewerbe Gruppe
Poster, Hannah Höch (1889-1978)
Germany, c. 1925. Lithograph

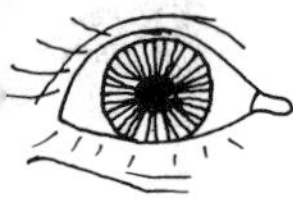

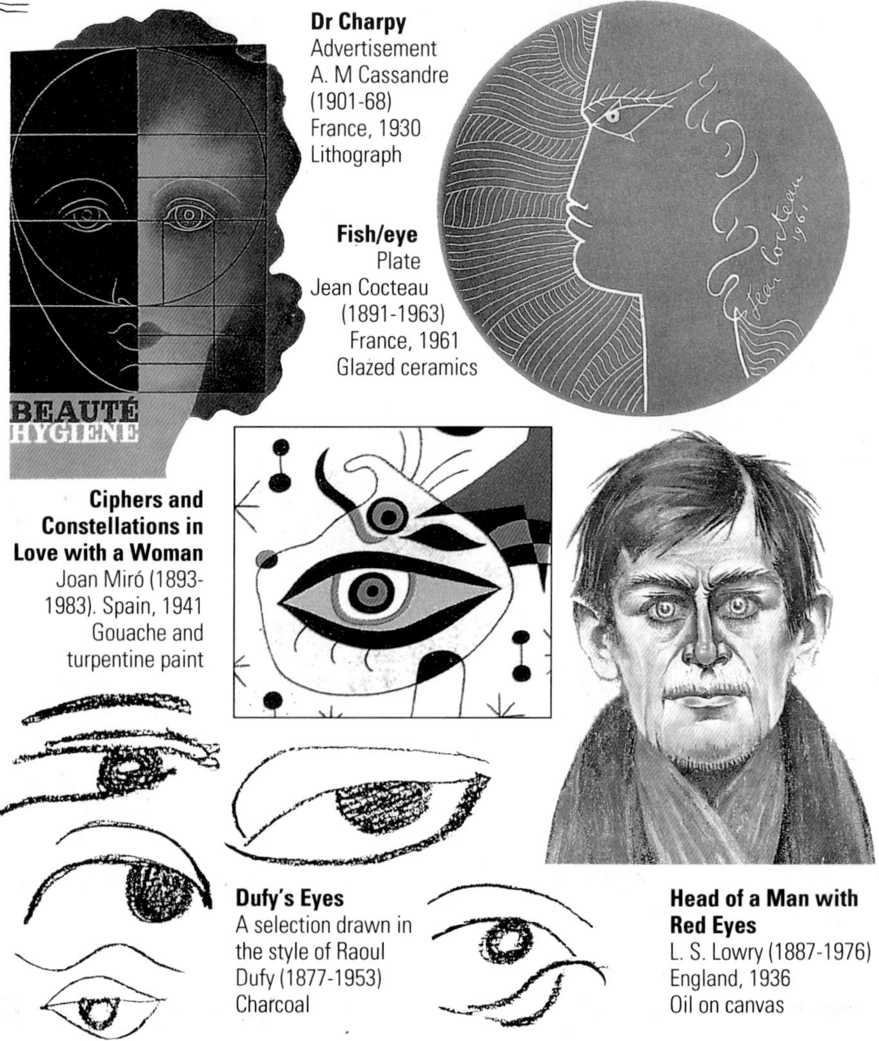

Dr Charpy
Advertisement
A. M Cassandre
(1901-68)
France, 1930
Lithograph

Fish/eye
Plate
Jean Cocteau
(1891-1963)
France, 1961
Glazed ceramics

Ciphers and Constellations in Love with a Woman
Joan Miró (1893-1983). Spain, 1941
Gouache and turpentine paint

Dufy's Eyes
A selection drawn in the style of Raoul Dufy (1877-1953)
Charcoal

Head of a Man with Red Eyes
L. S. Lowry (1887-1976)
England, 1936
Oil on canvas

Vicky
Detail
Roy Lichtenstein
(b. 1923). USA, 1964
Enamel on steel

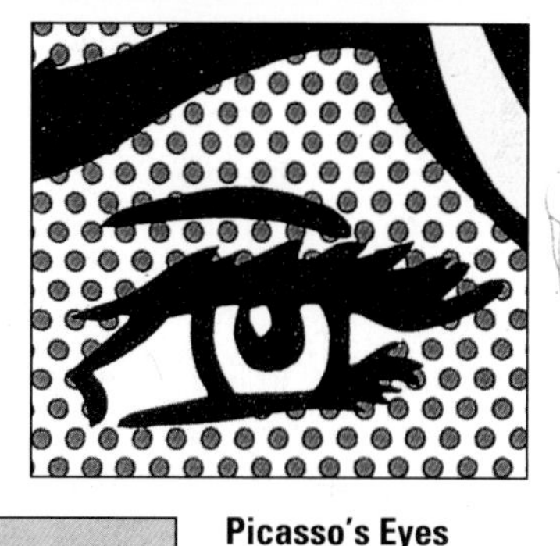

Self-portrait
Henri Matisse (1869-1954)
France, 1944. Pen and ink

Liz
Detail
Andy Warhol
(1930-87). USA, 1965
Silkscreen

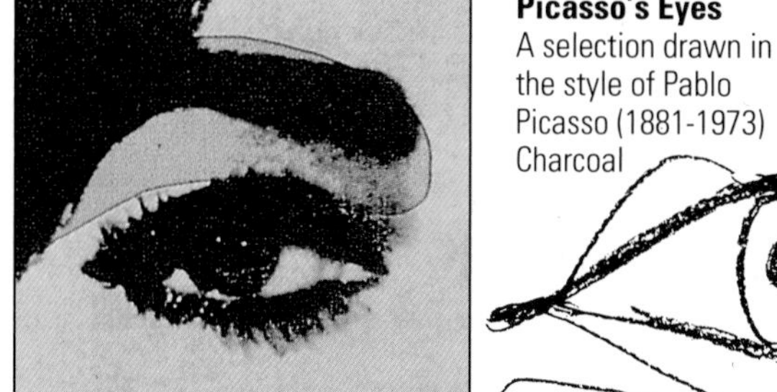

Picasso's Eyes
A selection drawn in
the style of Pablo
Picasso (1881-1973)
Charcoal

Fingerprint faces
G. Atler (b. 1946)
England, 1993
Pen and ink with ink
fingerprints

Image of Bhairava
Wall shrine
India, 1980s
Paint on stone

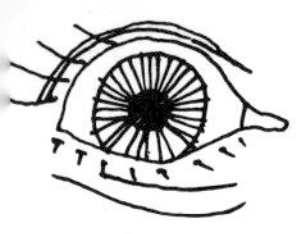

CONTRIBUTORS AND CONSULTANTS

Contributing artists

Roger Coleman is a portrait painter and illustrator whose work has been published in many books and magazines. He is the author of *Downland*, a book of writings and landscape paintings, and a former editor of *Design* magazine, the journal of the Design Center in London. He lectures frequently, and exhibits regularly at the Royal Academy and the Royal Watercolor Society in London.

Robin Harris qualified in Industrial Design at the Central School of Art in London, and was awarded a Royal Society of Arts travel bursary. He is a professional illustrator and designer whose work has appeared in many books, manuals, and magazines. He is a Fellow of the Royal Society of Arts, and a contributing artist to *Ways of Drawing Hands* in this series.

Educational consultant

Carolynn Cooke gained a degree in Graphic Design from Canterbury College of Art and a Postgraduate Certificate of Education from Leicester University. She has been teaching art for over twenty years, and is currently Head of Art and Design at Impington Village College, near Cambridge, England.

SOURCES/BIBLIOGRAPHY

In addition to the original artwork shown in this book, many books, journals, printed sources, galleries, and collections have been consulted in the preparation of this work. The following will be found to make useful and pleasurable reading in connection with the history and development of the art of drawing eyes:

Age of Chivalry,
J. Alexander and P. Binski, Royal Academy of Arts, 1987
Andy Warhol, K. Honnef, Benedikt Taschen, 1990
Arbanassi: Iconostases and Religious Easel Art,
S. Bossilkov, Svyat, 1989
An Atlas of Anatomy for Artists, F. Schider, Dover, 1957
Classical Greece, C. Bowra, Time-Life, 1966
"The Cocteau Hour,"
E. Thompson, in *Madame Figaro* magazine, October 1993
The Complete Encyclopedia of Illustration,
J. Heck, Merehurst Press, 1990
Drawings of the Holbein Family,
E. Schilling, Faber & Faber, 1937
Egon Schiele, F. Whitford, Thames & Hudson, 1981
The Encyclopedia of Comic Books,
R. Goulart, Time as Art, 1990
Eric Gill: The Engravings, C. Skelton, Herbert Press, 1990
The Greek Museums, Ekdotike Athenon S. A., 1975
The Great Collectors, V. Prat, Tabard Press, 1990
Joan Miró, W. Erben, Benedikt Taschen, 1988
Leonardo da Vinci, South Bank Center, 1989
The Letts Guide to Collecting Masks,
T. Teuten, Letts, 1990
Modigliani, C. Parisot, Pierre Terrail, 1992
Myths of Life and Death, T. Burland, Macmillan, 1974
The Paintings of L. S. Lowry, M. Levy, Jupiter, 1978
Pathway Icons: The Wayside Art of India,
P. Mookerjee, Thames & Hudson, 1987
Paul Klee: Figures and Faces,
M. Plant, Thames & Hudson, 1987
Portraits of the Artist: The Self-Portrait in Painting,
P. Bonafoux, Rizzoli, 1985
Primitive Art, L. Adam, Penguin, 1949
Roy Lichtenstein, J. Hendrickson, Benedikt Taschen, 1992
Twentieth-century Erotic Art,
G. Néret, Benedikt Taschen, 1993
The Twentieth-century Poster,
D. Ades, Abbeville Press, 1984
Verve 1937-60, M. Anthonioz, Abrams, 1988
Vincent van Gogh: Drawings, J. van der Wolk,
R. Pickvance, and E. Pey, Arnoldo Mondadori, 1990